P9-CRE-485

GREAT SYNAGOGUE
OF BUDAPEST

Jennifer Howse

www.av2books.com

AV² provides enriched content that supplements and complements this book. Weigl's AV² books strive to create inspired learning and engage young minds in a total learning experience.

Your AV² Media Enhanced books come alive with...

Audio
Listen to sections of the book read aloud.

Key Words
Study vocabulary, and complete a matching word activity.

Video
Watch informative video clips.

Quizzes
Test your knowledge.

Go to **www.av2books.com**, and enter this book's unique code.

Embedded Weblinks
Gain additional information for research.

Slide Show
View images and captions, and prepare a presentation.

BOOK CODE

Y747523

Try This!
Complete activities and hands-on experiments.

... and much, much more!

AV² by Weigl brings you media enhanced books that support active learning.

Published by AV² by Weigl
350 5th Avenue, 59th Floor
New York, NY 10118
Websites: www.av2books.com   www.weigl.com

Library of Congress Cataloging-in-Publication Data
Howse, Jennifer.
 The Great Synagogue of Budapest / Jennifer Howse.
    pages cm. -- (Houses of faith)
 Includes bibliographical references and index.
 ISBN 978-1-4896-2611-0 (hardcover : alk. paper) -- ISBN 978-1-4896-2615-8 (softcover : alk. paper) -- ISBN 978-1-4896-2619-6 (single-user ebk.) -- ISBN 978-1-4896-2623-3 (multi-user ebk.)
 1. Dohány Utcai Zsinagóga--Juvenile literature. 2. Synagogues--Hungary--Budapest--Juvenile literature. 3. Synagogue architecture--Hungary--Budapest--Juvenile literature. 4. Budapest (Hungary)--Buildings, structures, etc.--Juvenile literature. I. Title.
 NA5521.5.B825H69 2014
 726'.30943912--dc23
                    2014038683

Printed in the United States of America in North Mankato, Minnesota
1 2 3 4 5 6 7 8 9 0 18 17 16 15 14

112014
WEP311214

Editor: Heather Kissock
Design: Mandy Christiansen

Every reasonable effort has been made to trace ownership and to obtain permission to reprint copyright material. The publishers would be pleased to have any errors or omissions brought to their attention so that they may be corrected in subsequent printings. Weigl acknowledges Getty Images, Corbis, Alamy, Newscom, iStockphoto, and Dreamstime as its primary image suppliers for this title.

Contents

What Is the Great Synagogue?

The Jewish Quarter of Budapest, Hungary, is home to one of the largest **synagogues** in the world. Built in the mid-1800s, the Great Synagogue has remained a constant through difficult times. As many as 20,000 Jewish people sought refuge in the synagogue during the **Holocaust**. However, the synagogue was also occupied by **Nazi** forces for part of World War II. Although it survived the tumult, much work had to be done to restore the synagogue to its original state. Today, the Great Synagogue stands as a testament to the resilience of Budapest's Jewish community.

The synagogue's beginning was full of promise. Over the years, Budapest's Jewish population had been growing. From the late 1700s to the time of the 1857 census, the Jewish community had increased from about 300 people to more than 23,000. Jewish leaders recognized the need for a central place of worship. They began planning a grand synagogue that would showcase the strength of Budapest's Jewish community. This was to become the Great Synagogue.

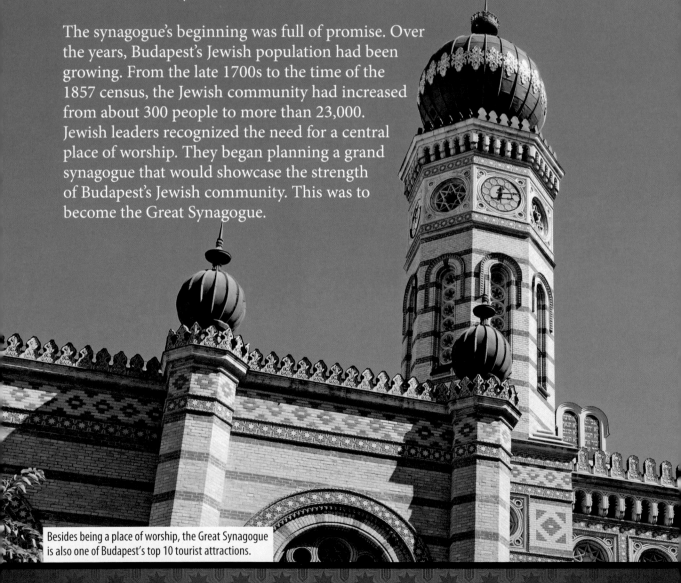

Besides being a place of worship, the Great Synagogue is also one of Budapest's top 10 tourist attractions.

The Jewish Faith

Judaism is one of the oldest religions in the world. It was founded by a man named Moses more than 3,500 years ago. Judaism is based on the teachings of the **Hebrew** Bible, or Old Testament. The first section of the Hebrew Bible is called the Torah. Jewish people consider the Torah to be the most important document of their faith. The Torah tells them how to behave and provides them with guidelines for living good lives. Jewish people go to synagogue to hear readings of the Torah. Readings are often performed by spiritual leaders called rabbis. It is their duty to understand and share the laws and traditions of Judaism with members of the synagogue.

There are more than

13 million
Jewish people worldwide.

Judaism is the **oldest** surviving monotheistic faith. This means that Jewish people believe there is only **one God**.

Top 5 Jewish Populations

Israel 5,900,000

United States 5,400,000

France 600,000

Canada 364,000

Great Britain 275,000

Approximately **1** in every **514** people is Jewish.

A Step Back in Time

The Great Synagogue began to take shape following the construction of another synagogue in Vienna, Austria. Completed in 1826, the Leopoldstadt Temple served as an example for the Jewish people of Budapest and encouraged them to begin building their own place of worship. A committee of community and religious leaders was formed. It was responsible for finding a location and deciding on an **architectural** plan.

The land for the synagogue was purchased in 1844. The process then began to determine the building's design. The committee received design ideas from three architects. It selected the plans of a German architect named Ludwig Förster.

CONSTRUCTION TIMELINE

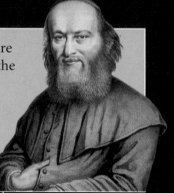

1826 The Jewish community in Budapest begins discussing plans to build a synagogue.

1844 Both plots are purchased so that the synagogue can be built. The building committee is established, led by Rabbi Löw Schwab.

1854 After selecting Ludwig Förster as the building's architect, the **cornerstone** for the new synagogue is placed on September 5.

| 1825 | 1835 | 1845 | 1855 | 1900 |

1837 The Jewish community begins renting the plot of land where the synagogue sits today. It rents a neighboring plot a few years later.

1859 The synagogue completes construction. The ceremonial opening takes place on September 6.

Förster planned a synagogue in the Moorish Revival style. This type of architecture reflects the design features of buildings in southern Spain. The Great Synagogue was to be as grand outside as it was inside. Construction on the synagogue began in 1854. It was another five years before it was completed.

Also called the Tempelgasse Synagogue, Vienna's Leopoldstadt Temple was one of the masterpiece buildings designed by Ludwig Förster. The synagogue was destroyed in 1938 during anti-Jewish riots.

1930
Construction begins on a new building beside the synagogue. Upon completion a year later, it becomes the home of the new Jewish Museum. It is later attached to the synagogue.

1940s During World War II, Nazi forces use the synagogue as a communications center and stable.

1950s Following the war, the building is boarded up to protect it from further damage.

1930	1940	1950	1990	2000

1939 The synagogue is bombed by Nazi supporters.

1991 A large-scale restoration of the synagogue begins. It is completed in 1996.

The Great Synagogue's Location

The Great Synagogue is also known as the Dohány Synagogue. This is because it sits on Budapest's Dohány Street, which serves as an entrance to the city's Jewish district. The street is considered the center of Hungary's Jewish community.

WIDTH At its widest point, the synagogue measures 87 feet (26.5 meters) across.

LENGTH The synagogue is 173 feet (52.7 m) long.

The Great Synagogue was built in a residential area. Today, the area remains residential but also has a number of shops and restaurants for locals and tourists to visit.

Over the years, other structures have been built around the synagogue, creating a much larger complex. The Jewish Museum stands adjacent to the synagogue. Behind the synagogue is the Heroes' Memorial Temple. This structure honors the Jewish soldiers who died in World War I.

★Budapest

HUNGARY

N

0   250 Miles
0   250 Kilometers

HEIGHT The synagogue's towers are its highest points. They reach 141 feet (43 m) into the sky. The clock faces on each tower have a **diameter** of 4.4 feet (1.3 m).

AREA The interior floor space covers 3,280 square feet (305 square m).

Outside the Great Synagogue

The Great Synagogue's design is mostly in the Moorish Revival style. However, influences from other design styles can also be seen in its architecture.

TOWERS The synagogue's two towers rise up above the front entrance. Constructed in the **Byzantine**-Moorish style, each tower is topped with an onion-shaped dome. Curving **gold leaf** crests have been placed around the middle of each dome. Two stone tablets sit on the roof between the domes. Written in gold on the tablets are the Ten Commandments.

OUTER WALLS The exterior of the synagogue is covered in yellow and red bricks, with a row of floral-patterned **crenels** running along the top of the walls. Ceramics have been used to decorate the walls in the Moorish style. Patterns created from the ceramics include eight-point stars, flowers, and various **geometric** designs.

MAIN ENTRANCE The main entrance to the synagogue is framed by an **arch**. People walk through this archway to get to a smaller arch that contains the door to the synagogue. This smaller archway is topped by an eight-point star enclosed in a circle. A Hebrew **inscription** sits above the main entrance. It features a quote from the Bible. The date of the building's completion is also found above the entrance.

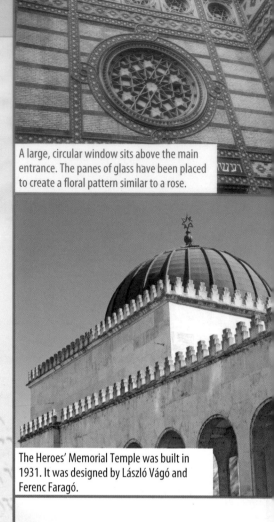

A large, circular window sits above the main entrance. The panes of glass have been placed to create a floral pattern similar to a rose.

The Heroes' Memorial Temple was built in 1931. It was designed by László Vágó and Ferenc Faragó.

The Tree of Life Holocaust Memorial is located at the back of the synagogue. Each of the tree's metal leaves holds the name of a Hungarian of Jewish faith who died during the Holocaust.

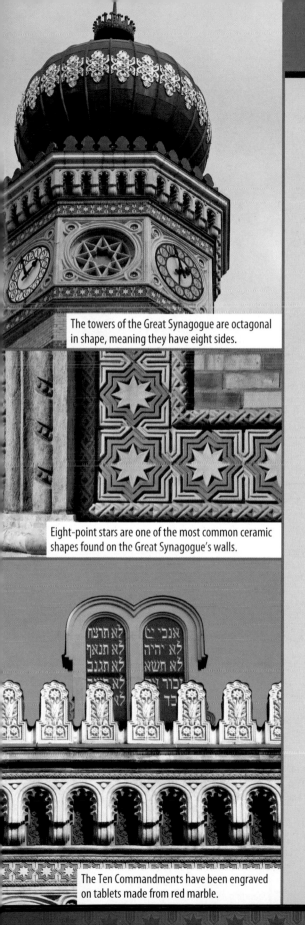

The towers of the Great Synagogue are octagonal in shape, meaning they have eight sides.

Eight-point stars are one of the most common ceramic shapes found on the Great Synagogue's walls.

The Ten Commandments have been engraved on tablets made from red marble.

The Great Synagogue is the **LARGEST** synagogue in Europe.

None of the four clocks on the towers actually work.

Cosmetics maven Estée Lauder donated **$5 million** to help restore the synagogue.

During World War II, the synagogue was **bombed 27 times**.

Budapest has **26** active synagogues.

The Great Synagogue and two other nearby synagogues form **Budapest's Synagogue Triangle.**

Inside the Great Synagogue

The interior of the Great Synagogue is known for its grandeur. Colorful artwork, sparkling chandeliers, and clustered columns create an ornate vision.

GALLERIES It is Jewish tradition for women and men to be separated during prayer service. Two-story **galleries** run along each side of the synagogue. The women's seating is in the second-story galleries. The galleries are supported by delicate, slender pillars. These pillars are topped with light fixtures shaped like trees. Chandeliers of a similar design hang from the ceiling.

ARK An important feature of the synagogue is the Ark. This structure serves as a cabinet in which to store the Torah. The Ark in the Great Synagogue contains the synagogue's own Torah scroll, along with 25 others. These scrolls were saved from synagogues that were destroyed during World War II. The Ark is found on the synagogue's eastern wall. This is an important position in the synagogue as it is the wall closest to Jerusalem.

DOME Above the Ark is a **pendentive** dome. The top of the dome features a stained glass window which lets in natural light. The window's design consists of a large eight-point star surrounded by several smaller stars. The dome's interior is painted in the Moorish style, with **filigree** swirls of blue and gold.

A lantern hangs above the Ark. It features the Star of David, a symbol important to the Jewish faith.

The Torah is written on a scroll. Only certain people are allowed to write the Torah. Called sofers, they are specially trained to write and assemble the scroll.

Special services at the Great Synagogue can attract as many as 5,000 worshippers. The synagogue seats about 3,000 and has standing room for another 2,000.

Each of the large chandeliers contains 124 light bulbs.

Stained glass windows run along the ceiling of the synagogue. They act like a skylight by allowing natural light into the building.

Two gold candelabras stand on either side of the Ark, while the *bimah*, or Torah table, sits in front. It is here that the Torah is placed and read during services.

Women **MUST** cover their shoulders before entering the synagogue.

Each of the large chandeliers weighs

1.2 tons
(1.1 metric tons).

The Ark is
26 feet
(7.9 m) high.

Composer Franz Liszt played the organ at the
1859
opening of the Great Synagogue.

1,492 seats are reserved for men.

1,472 seats are set aside for women.

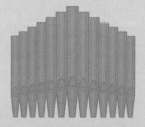

The synagogue's organ has **4,500** pipes.

The Science behind the Great Synagogue

The Great Synagogue was constructed in the 19th century. The architects and builders of the Great Synagogue used the most up-to-date technologies for that time to create the building. To achieve the soaring heights and the shape of the structure, techniques were used that required knowledge of **engineering** and science.

CASTING IRON Cast iron arches span the Great Synagogue's **nave**, providing support to the ceiling. Cast iron is metal that can be shaped using casts, or molds. There are several steps involved in making cast iron. The process begins by melting **iron ore** in a blast furnace. Once melted, it is poured into cubed molds called pigs. The pigs are then melted, and a combination of **alloys** and scrap metal are added to the liquid. This liquid is then poured into casts to create the shapes and structures required.

ARCHES Arches are found throughout the Great Synagogue. They are used to frame windows, form entrances, and support the ceiling. Architects have relied on arches for centuries. Arches are used to support heavy weights. An arch supports the weight of a building by converting the downward force of the weight into an outward force. The outward force spreads the weight of the structure evenly across a larger area. In the case of the Great Synagogue, the arch shifts the downward force of the building away from the windows, entrances, and nave that they frame.

THE PROPERTIES OF GOLD The Great Synagogue has several ornamental features that have been made from gold. Gold is one of the most **malleable** metals. It is often pounded into thin sheets called gold plate. Gold can be used on the exterior or interior of buildings as a long-lasting covering. This is because it does not **corrode** or break down like other metals. Gold-plated ornaments were placed on the towers' onion domes because they could face all kinds of weather, including wind, rain, snow, and sunlight, without being degraded.

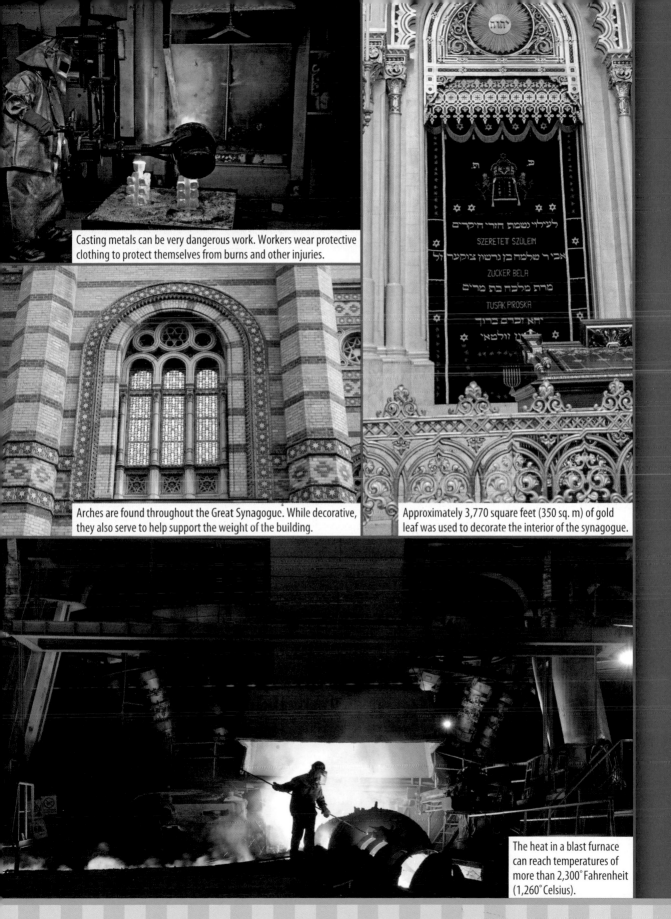

Casting metals can be very dangerous work. Workers wear protective clothing to protect themselves from burns and other injuries.

Arches are found throughout the Great Synagogue. While decorative, they also serve to help support the weight of the building.

Approximately 3,770 square feet (350 sq. m) of gold leaf was used to decorate the interior of the synagogue.

The heat in a blast furnace can reach temperatures of more than 2,300°Fahrenheit (1,260°Celsius).

The Great Synagogue's Builders

The Great Synagogue was built due to the efforts of a number of people. Each had a vision for a synagogue that would properly represent a people and their faith. Planners, architects, designers, and builders worked diligently toward this goal.

Löw Schwab Rabbi Löw Schwab was born at Krumau in Moravia, in 1794. He received his early schooling privately and enrolled in the Nikolsburg **yeshiva** at age 11 to advance his Judaic studies. He was ordained as a rabbi in 1828. Schwab moved to Budapest in 1836 and quickly began working toward strengthening its Jewish community. Schwab believed strongly in education and encouraged the community to build schools for their young children. He also played a key role in bringing the first Jewish hospital to the area. Even though he did not live to see its completion, the Great Synagogue remains his greatest legacy to the people of Hungary.

Ludwig Förster Born in Ansbach, Germany, in 1797, Förster was educated in both Germany and Austria. His studies in Germany included two years of art school. Upon moving to Austria, Förster became a respected teacher at Vienna's Academy of Fine Arts, where he taught from 1842 to 1845. A very prolific architect, Förster created plans for houses, palaces, and apartment buildings. He also worked on public buildings such as schools and churches. His designs had a great effect on the appearance of the cities of Vienna and Budapest.

Frigyes Feszl had been one of the three architects to submit a design concept for the synagogue in 1854. When Ludwig Förster was unavailable to help with the construction, Ignác Wechselmann asked Feszl to complete the interior.

Ignác Wechselmann Ignác Wechselmann was the master builder in charge of the construction of the Great Synagogue. Wechselmann was born in Prussia in 1828 and received his education in Berlin, Germany. He then moved to Vienna, where he became an assistant to Ludwig Förster. Wechselmann was the first Jewish member of the Hungarian Master Builders' Guild, and from the 1850s to 1890s, was involved in the construction of some of the most important buildings in Hungary. In 1886, he received the Order of the Iron Crown from Austria's emperor Franz Joseph I for his service to the country. In 1890, Wechselmann had to retire due to failing eyesight. When he died in 1903, his will left funding to build a school for the visually impaired.

Frigyes Feszl Much of the Great Synagogue's interior was designed by the architect Frigyes Feszl. Born in Budapest in 1821, he was the son of a master **stonemason**. Feszl received his early schooling in Budapest, but later moved to Munich, Germany, and Paris, France, to continue his studies in art and architecture. Upon his return to Hungary, he soon established himself as one of the leading designers of the Hungarian Romantic movement. This was a style of design that featured ornate decorative features. The **frescoes**, chandeliers, and ceiling decoration in the Great Synagogue are all a result of Feszl's Romantic style. Similar design elements can also be seen in Budapest's Municipal Concert Hall, which Feszl designed in 1858.

Similar Structures around the World

When Ludwig Förster decided to apply the Moorish Revival style to the Jewish synagogues he designed, he said that it was because there was no clearly defined European Jewish architectural style. The style proved to be popular with the Jewish community and was adopted for many of the synagogues that followed.

Grand Choral Synagogue

BUILT: 1880–1893
LOCATION: St. Petersburg, Russia
DESIGN: L. Bakhman and I. Shaposhnikov
DESCRIPTION: The Grand Choral Synagogue is Europe's second largest synagogue, after the Great Synagogue of Budapest. It was built to give the Jewish people of St. Petersburg a central place of worship. Covering approximately 34,445 square feet (3,200 sq. m), it can house up to 1,200 people. There is one central men's section surrounded by three seating areas for women. Besides the **sanctuary**, the synagogue also has a wedding hall, a bakery and restaurant, and a school.

The Grand Choral Synagogue recently underwent a $5 million restoration, which was completed in 2005.

Central Synagogue

BUILT: 1872
LOCATION: New York City, New York, United States
DESIGN: Henry Fernbach
DESCRIPTION: The Central Synagogue is the oldest synagogue in New York in continuous use. It was built to accommodate the growing number of Jewish immigrants arriving in New York in the 1800s. The synagogue features two domed towers similar to the ones on Budapest's Great Synagogue. The exterior and interior decorations are also based on the design of the Budapest building. The nave is divided into three sections, and there are two levels of galleries. Cast iron pillars divide the space into six sections. Golden domes and **gilded** stars make the Central Synagogue of New York a unique and beautiful building.

The Central Synagogue was designated a National Historic Landmark in 1975.

The Spanish Synagogue ceased to be a place of worship during World War II. It was only reopened to the public in 1998, on the 130th anniversary of its establishment.

Spanish Synagogue

BUILT: 1868
LOCATION: Prague, Czech Republic
DESIGN: Vojtěch Ignátz Ullmann
DESCRIPTION: The Spanish Synagogue was built on the site where Prague's oldest house of prayer once stood. Its design is based on a square. In the center of the square is a high dome. The nave is surrounded on three sides by galleries that are supported by metal structures. Similar to the Great Synagogue of Budapest, the walls, doors, and railings of the Spanish Synagogue are decorated in the Moorish Revival design style. Stained glass windows allow natural light to shine into the building.

Issues Facing the Great Synagogue

Buildings that represent a community are important to the culture and history of its members. Preserving these buildings over long periods of time is necessary. It can, however, be an expensive and often difficult task. The Great Synagogue of Budapest is a marvel of architecture, but it also served as a refuge, became a derelict building, and is now a re-built historical site.

WHAT IS THE ISSUE?

The building was almost destroyed by the ravages of war and neglect.	The synagogue lacked modern technology.

EFFECTS

Paint had chipped and faded. Ornamental decorations had become worn and discolored. The roof was in danger of collapse.	Electrical systems were outdated. Lighting was not energy efficient.

ACTION TAKEN

As part of a large-scale restoration plan, the roof has been reinforced and restored, surfaces repainted, and gold ornaments replated.	A modern heating system has been installed. Light fixtures are now equipped with energy-saving light bulbs.

Make an Eight-Point Star

One of the most beautiful and interesting parts of the Great Synagogue of Budapest is its Moorish designs. These designs twist and turn around the main entrance and are also seen in other parts of the building. The most prominent design in the synagogue is the eight-point star. You can create your own eight-point star following the instructions below.

Materials
- 8 sheets of origami paper
- glue or scotch tape

Instructions

1. Fold one sheet of paper in half to make a rectangle. Crease and open the paper.

2. Make the same fold using the other sides of the paper. Crease and open the paper. The creases should now form a cross on the paper.

3. Fold the paper in half diagonally. Crease and open the paper.

4. Turn the paper so that one of the points is turned toward you. Fold the left corner so that the tip meets the center line. Crease the paper, and leave it folded. Repeat this step with the corner on the right side of the paper.

5. Returning to the left side of the paper, fold the bottom point in to meet the center line. Crease the paper, and leave it folded. Repeat on the right side. You now have one of your star's eight points.

6. Repeat steps 1 through 5 using the other seven sheets of paper.

7. Place the eight sheets of paper face down, and glue or tape them together. Turn the sheets over to admire your eight-point star.

Great Synagogue Quiz

Q Who designed the Great Synagogue?

A Ludwig Förster

Q What purpose does the Ark serve?

A It is where the Torah is kept.

Q What is another name for the Great Synagogue?

A Dohány Synagogue

Q Which architectural style was used in the design of the synagogue?

A Moorish Revival

Key Words

alloys: substances made from two or more metals

arch: a curved structure that spans an opening and supports a roof or wall

architectural: related to the design of buildings and other structures

Byzantine: relating to the Byzantine empire, which spanned much of southern Europe and Asia during the Middle Ages

cornerstone: the first stone laid in a structure

corrode: to wear away gradually

crenels: indented sections along the top of a wall

diameter: the length of a line that passes through the center of a circle from one side to the other

engineering: the application of scientific and mathematical principles to construct buildings and other structures

filigree: delicate and complex designs made from wire

frescoes: paintings on plaster surfaces

galleries: upper stories that project from the wall and are supported by columns

geometric: of or related to basic lines and shapes

gilded: covered with a thin layer of gold

gold leaf: gold powder that has been applied to a surface

Hebrew: the ancient language of the Jewish people

Holocaust: the killing of millions of Jewish and other people during World War II

inscription: words that are carved into a surface

iron ore: a rock or mineral from which iron can be taken

malleable: can be stretched or bent into different shapes

nave: the central space in a religious building

Nazi: a member of a political party that controlled Germany from 1933 to 1945

pendentive: a circular support for a dome

sanctuary: the room inside a religious building where services are held

stonemason: a person skilled in building with stone

synagogues: religious buildings where Jewish people meet to worship

yeshiva: a Jewish college

Index

Log on to www.av2books.com

AV² by Weigl brings you media enhanced books that support active learning. Go to www.av2books.com, and enter the special code found on page 2 of this book. You will gain access to enriched and enhanced content that supplements and complements this book. Content includes video, audio, weblinks, quizzes, a slide show, and activities.

AV² Online Navigation

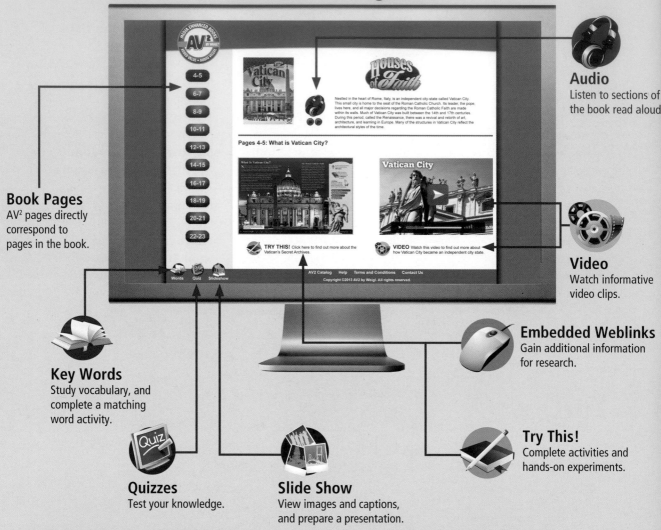

Book Pages
AV² pages directly correspond to pages in the book.

Audio
Listen to sections of the book read aloud.

Video
Watch informative video clips.

Key Words
Study vocabulary, and complete a matching word activity.

Embedded Weblinks
Gain additional information for research.

Quizzes
Test your knowledge.

Slide Show
View images and captions, and prepare a presentation.

Try This!
Complete activities and hands-on experiments.

AV² was built to bridge the gap between print and digital. We encourage you to tell us what you like and what you want to see in the future.

Sign up to be an AV² Ambassador at www.av2books.com/ambassador.